Positive
Sermon
Outlines

Positive Sermon Outlines

Russell E. Spray

BAKER BOOK HOUSE
Grand Rapids, Michigan 49516

Copyright © 1991 by Baker Books
a division of Baker Book House Company
P.O. Box 6287, Grand Rapids, MI 49516-6287

ISBN: 0-8010-8318-4

Sixth printing, January 1999

Printed in the United States of America

For information about books, resources for Christian leaders, and all new releases available from Baker Book House, visit our web site:
                    http://www.bakerbooks.com/

Contents

Preface

Positive Sermon Outlines is designed to assist busy ministers with their sermon preparation. I trust these messages will inspire an optimistic outlook and encourage Christians in their quest for a closer walk with God. I also hope that they will cause the unsaved to seek and find Christ as their Savior and Lord. My prayer is that God's blessings will be on all who use and hear these sermon outlines.

Russell E. Spray

1

Be a Positive Person

"Let this mind be in you, which was also in Christ Jesus"
(Phil. 2:5).

I. Think Positive Thoughts

"Whatsoever things are of good report . . . think on these things" (Phil. 4:8).
A. Some Christians fail to discipline their thinking. They allow negatives to dominate their minds.
B. Christians must take deliberate action, replacing negative thoughts with positives and keeping an optimistic outlook.

II. Hear Positive Sounds

"And it was revealed in mine ears by the LORD" (Isa. 22:14).
A. Many people listen to the filth, smut, and destruction coming across the airwaves. Their spirits are dwarfed.
B. We must listen to the good, not the bad. We must hear from the Lord and heed his Word.

III. See Positive Sights

"Looking unto Jesus the author and finisher of our faith . . ." (Heb. 12:2).
A. Some Christians look for the bad in people and circumstances, seeing only the faults and negatives.
B. To be a positive person one must look for the good and look to Jesus.

IV. Speak Positive Words

"Talk ye of all his wondrous works" (Ps. 105:2).
A. Many people talk mostly about evil and bad events. Some are harsh, unkind, and take God's name in vain.
B. We should talk positively, seeking to glorify God by extolling his goodness, grace, and love.

V. Perform Positive Deeds

"And whatsoever ye do, do it heartily, as to the Lord, and not unto men" (Col. 3:23).
A. The deeds of many are negative. They are selfishly motivated, dishonest, and displeasing to God.
B. We must be truthful, ready to lift those who are down, and witness for Christ.

VI. Attend Positive Places

"I was glad when they said . . . Let us go into the house of the LORD" (Ps. 122:1).
A. Christians hurt their influence when they go to the wrong places in search of entertainment.
B. Be a positive Christian. Attend church faithfully. Go with God and he will go with you.

2

Beat the B-L-U-E-S

"Why art thou cast down, O my soul? and why art thou dis-quieted in me? hope thou in God: for I shall yet praise him" (Ps. 42:5).

Christians can beat the B-L-U-E-S if they:

I. B-elieve the Positive

"Whatsoever things are of good report . . . think on these things" (Phil. 4:8).
A. Too many Christians believe negatives rather than posi-tives. They look for, listen to, and concentrate on all the bad things that happen.
B. Contrarily, we should dwell on positives, looking for the good in others and circumstances.

II. L-ook for the Purpose

"After that ye have suffered a while . . . stablish, strengthen, settle you" (1 Peter 5:10).
A. God has a purpose for his people in all he allows. We win over discouragement by looking for his purpose.
B. Sometimes Christians are tested to strengthen and increase their faith. God promised to "strengthen."

III. U-tilize the Promises

" . . . that we through patience and comfort of the scriptures might have hope" (Rom. 15:4).
A. Some Christians lack victory because they neglect God's

promises, thus forfeiting many benefits promised in God's Word.

B. We must utilize God's promises by reading them, remembering them, and referring to them often.

IV. E-ncourage Other People

" . . . that we may be able to comfort them which are in any trouble . . ." (2 Cor. 1:4).

A. Many people fall into discouragement because they fail to help those who are in need. They are too involved with selfish pursuits.

B. We should encourage others by reaching out to help them with their problems. This often enables us to solve our own difficulties.

V. S-ing God's Praises

"Sing forth the honour of his name: make his praise glorious" (Ps. 66:2).

A. Most Christians fail to praise the Lord enough. Praising God brings hope. It helps lift us out of despair.

B. The psalmist said, "But I will hope continually, and will yet praise thee more and more" (Ps. 71:14).

3

Biblical Promises for Today

"Whereby are given unto us exceeding great and precious promises: that by these ye might be partakers of the divine nature" (2 Peter 1:4).

I. The Bible Promises Pardon That Converts

"Repent . . . and be converted, that your sins may be blotted out" (Acts 3:19).
A. God's pardoning grace converts our will, ways, work, and walk. "Old things are passed away" (2 Cor. 5:17).
B. We must come to God just as we are in simple, trusting faith (Eph. 2:8).
C. God's amazing grace is sufficient to forgive all—adulterers, homosexuals, drug abusers—who repent and forsake their sins.

II. The Bible Promises Purity That Cleanses

" . . . giving them the Holy Ghost . . . purifying their hearts by faith" (Acts 15:8, 9).
A. Many Christians do not commit their will totally to God. They reserve a portion for selfish endeavor.
B. When Christians totally surrender to God, the blood of Jesus Christ cleanses their hearts (*see* 1 John 1:7).
C. Cleansed Christians are filled with God's love. They glorify him and are a blessing to others.

III. The Bible Promises Peace That Calms

"And the peace of God . . . shall keep your hearts and minds through Christ Jesus" (Phil. 4:7).

A. Today's world is searching desperately for peace, but to no avail. More conflict, stress, and strain abound than ever before.
B. Peace can only be found in Jesus Christ. He promised, "My peace I give unto you . . . let not your heart be troubled" (John 14:27).
C. Christ's peace calms those who trust in him. To have his peace, we must simply accept the peace that he gives.

IV. The Bible Promises Power That Conquers

"But ye shall receive power, after that the Holy Ghost is come upon you: and ye shall be witnesses unto me" (Acts 1:8).

A. Spirit-filled Christians are endued with power for service. They are ready to comfort the lonely, assist the homeless, and witness for Christ.
B. The Spirit-filled are diligent in prayer and Bible study. They are enabled to overcome trials, troubles, and tribulations, and to become victorious over sin, self, and Satan.
C. The Scripture promises: "Nay, in all these things we are more than conquerors" (Rom. 8:37).

4

Conquer with God's Word

"Thy word have I hid in mine heart, that I might not sin against thee" (Ps. 119:11).

I. Discover God's Word

"Blessed art thou, O LORD: teach me thy statutes" (Ps. 119:12).

A. The psalmist asked God to teach him his Word. We should do likewise.

B. Discovering God's promises means finding those that apply to our area of need. A good concordance and reference Bible help us locate them.

C. We discover God's Word when we trust him to reveal it to us.

II. Digest God's Word

"Open thou mine eyes, that I may behold wondrous things out of thy law" (Ps. 119:18).

A. Webster says that *digest* means "to think over and absorb."

B. We need to delve into God's promises, studying and pondering them. (Good commentaries help.)   Let us absorb God's Word until we are absorbed by it.

C. Partake of God's Word. Digest it. The psalmist wrote "O taste and see that the LORD is good" (Ps. 34:8).

III. Delight in God's Word

"And I will delight myself in thy commandments, which I have loved" (Ps. 119:47).

A. Some do not delight in God's Word. Reading it is a duty to be performed. Their negative attitude brings spiritual defeat.
B. Delighting in God's Word enables us to be conquerors. "They are the rejoicing of my heart," said the psalmist (Ps. 119:111).
C. Christians who delight in God's Word love his Word, obey his Word, and are victorious through his Word. Let us claim the promises with praise (*see* Ps. 119:165).

IV. Depend on God's Word

"For ever, O Lord, thy word is settled in heaven" (Ps. 119:89).

A. Many Christians do not depend on God's Word as they should. They rely on self-effort or other people too much—and thereby fail.
B. If we are to conquer, we must depend on God's Word. It never fails. "There hath not failed one word of all his good promise" (1 Kings 8:56).
C. Few things in this life are trustworthy. Possessions fail, pleasures fade, popularity falls, and people falter. "But the word of the Lord endureth for ever" (1 Peter 1:25).

5

Dynamics of Love

"And I pray that you, being rooted and established in love, may have power . . . to grasp how wide and long and high and deep is the love of Christ" (Eph. 3:17, 18 NIV).

Christians can increase in love by considering:

I. The Source of Love

"God is love" (1 John 4:8, 16).
A. Much of the so-called love talked about in today's world is not true love at all. God is the source of real and lasting love. His love is pure and holy.
B. God is also the source of his Word. He spoke his Word to faithful men who recorded it diligently. "All scripture is given by inspiration of God" (2 Tim. 3:16).
C. God's Word teaches us about God's love. It tells of the sacrifice of his own Son "for his great love wherewith he loved us" (Eph. 2:4). We can accept God's love today through Jesus Christ.

II. The Force of Love

"He is able to save them to the uttermost that come unto God by him" (Heb. 7:25).
A. Today's world offers horse power, steam power, and nuclear power. None of these compare with the power of God's love.
B. Earthly power assists in easing the burdens of life, but it can also destroy life and bring devastation. The force of God's love brings peace and joy in this life and eternal life in the hereafter.

C. The power of God's love reaches everyone. It touches the gambler, thief, adulterer, prostitute, and homosexual. All who repent, believe, and forsake their sins may be saved (*see* John 3:15).

III. The Course of Love

"God so loved the world" (John 3:16).
A. God's love reaches into all the world. It touches young and old, the weak and strong, the great and small, and the rich and poor. Every race, color, and creed is included.
B. The love of many Christians is stymied because they are too busy with personal pursuits, or they are simply unconcerned about others. Their love does not reach out to others as it should.
C. Our love may touch others when we give a smile, speak a kind or encouraging word, perform a good deed by assisting the less fortunate, or by sharing Christ with the unsaved. "Go ye into all the world" (Mark 16:15).

6

Emulate the Love of God

"As the Father hath loved me, so have I loved you: continue ye in my love" (John 15:9).

God's love is:

I. Tough Love

"The Lord disciplines those he loves" (Heb. 12:6 NIV).

A. The Lord disciplines his children because he loves them and wants the best for them. He is looking out for their good (*see* Rom. 8:28 NIV).

B. We should thank God for his discipline because he is omniscient.

C. We can emulate God's love by displaying tough love also. We should discipline our children with firmness and love and work courageously for the good of others.

II. Tender Love

"For thy lovingkindness is good: turn unto me according to . . . thy tender mercies" (Ps. 69:16).

A. God's love is not only tough but it is also tender. He cares, understands, and "is touched with the feeling of our infirmities" (Heb. 4:15).

B. God's love, mercy, and grace are extended to all people in all places, at all times.

C. Emulate God's tender love. Heed his words: "Be ye kind one to another, tenderhearted, forgiving one another" (Eph. 4:32).

III. Trustworthy Love

"I have loved thee with an everlasting love" (Jer. 31:3).
A. Today's society is sadly lacking when it comes to trustworthy love. Divorce rates continually rise.
B. God's love is trustworthy. He keeps his promises (*see* Eph. 2:7).
C. We should be steadfast and dependable also, loving "in deed and in truth" (1 John 3:18).

IV. Triumphant Love

"Charity [love] never faileth" (1 Cor. 13:8).
A. People, possessions, pleasures, and popularity fail, but God's triumphant love never fails.
B. Before we can emulate God's triumphant love, we need to possess his love. We must totally commit ourselves to God to be filled with his love.
C. God's love is triumphant because "God is love" (1 John 4:8, 16). His love brings victory now and eternally. "The greatest of these is love" (1 Cor. 13:13 NIV).

7

Exercise Increases Strength

"For physical training is of some value, but godliness has value for all things, holding promise for both the present life and the life to come" (1 Tim. 4:8 NIV).

I. Exercise Increases Physical Strength

"For physical training is of some value" (1 Tim. 4:8 NIV).
A. Physical exercise is needed more today than ever because of the wear and tear of our present-day society. Stress and strain deplete our energy.
B. Exercise relaxes tense muscles, encourages healthy blood flow, and prevents heart and lung problems. It increases strength and often improves one's looks.
C. Millions of people are now aware of the value of exercise. Doctors recommend daily walking, bicycle riding, and other forms of working out.
D. God's Word teaches that our bodies are the temples of the Holy Spirit. "If any man defile the temple of God, him shall God destroy" (1 Cor. 3:17).

II. Exercise Increases Mental Strength

"Study to shew thyself approved unto God, a workman that needeth not to be ashamed, rightly dividing the word of truth" (2 Tim. 2:15).
A. World and national leaders are aware of the need for education. Our own president wants to be known as "The Education President."
B. Increasing mental power means reading, writing, and

learning. Just as physical exercise increases bodily strength, mental exercise increases mental strength.

C. Exercise in the study of God's Word is needed most. Not only must we believe his Word, but we must learn to rightly divide "the word of truth" (2 Tim. 2:15).

D. All who repent and forsake their sins may learn discipline and direction and receive deliverance through God's Word.

III. Exercise Increases Spiritual Strength

"But . . . exercise thyself rather unto godliness" (1 Tim. 4:7).

A. Physical and mental strength are received when we flex our physical and mental muscles. Spiritual strength is gained by flexing our spiritual muscles.

B. We gain spiritual strength as we wait on God in prayer and claim his promises.

C. We become hale and hearty Christians as we increase in the fruits of the Spirit: "love, joy, peace, longsuffering, gentleness, goodness, faith, meekness, temperance" (Gal. 5:22, 23).

8

Explaining God's G-R-A-C-E

"Let us therefore come boldly unto the throne of grace, that we may obtain mercy, and find grace to help in time of need" *(Heb. 4:16).*

I. G-reat Grace

"And great grace was upon them all" (Acts 4:33).
A. Webster defines *grace* as "the unmerited love and favor of God toward men."
B. God's grace is great because it brings pardon, purity, peace, and purpose to our life. We deserved to die in our sins but God's grace brought life through Jesus Christ (*see* Eph. 2:8).

II. R-edeeming Grace

"By grace ye are saved" (Eph. 2:5).
A. Because of God's redeeming grace, we must repent, believe, and be saved. Christ paid the supreme price for our sins.
B. The Scripture says, "That being justified by his grace, we should be made heirs . . . of eternal life" (Titus 3:7).

III. A-bundant Grace

"And God is able to make all grace abound unto you; that ye . . . may abound to every good work" (2 Cor. 9:8).
A. There are many shortages in our society. Many homeless people lack enough food to survive.
B. There is no shortage of God's grace. His Word calls it

"abundant grace." It renews the inward man day by day (*see* 2 Cor. 4:15, 16).

IV. C-omforting Grace

"And he said unto me, My grace is sufficient for thee: for my strength is made perfect in weakness" (2 Cor. 12:9).
A. Paul referred to his thorn in the flesh as a messenger of Satan. Instead of removing it, God assured him of sufficient grace and strength.
B. God allows us, like Paul, to be tested and tried to strengthen our faith. With Paul we can say, "When I am weak, then am I strong" (2 Cor. 12:10).

V. E-verlasting Grace

"That in the ages to come he might shew the exceeding riches of his grace" (Eph. 2:7).
A. Few things in today's world are lasting. Time takes its toll on our possessions and treasures.
B. God's grace is everlasting. It is great, redeeming, abundant, comforting, and enduring (*see* Eph. 2:7).

9

Follow the Example of Christ

" . . . leaving us an example, that we should follow his steps"
(1 Peter 2:21).

I. Christ Is Unselfish

"But God commendeth his love toward us, in that, while we were yet sinners, Christ died for us" (Rom. 5:8).
A. We deserved to die for our sins, "for the wages of sin is death" (Rom. 6:23). Christ took our sins on himself, giving his life in our stead.
B. We must deny ourselves and live for Christ and others (*see* Matt. 16:24).

II. Christ Is Understanding

"The LORD pitieth them that fear him. For he knoweth our frame; he remembereth that we are dust" (Ps. 103:13, 14).
A. When Christ was here on earth, he had great compassion on the sick, lame, blind, and sinful. He is the same today (*see* Heb.13:8).
B. Christ understands and cares about our infirmities and needs. We should also be understanding, caring for the less fortunate, needy, and sinful.

III. Christ Is Unfailing

"And the LORD, he it is that doth go before thee; he will be with thee, he will not fail thee, neither forsake thee" (Deut. 31:8).
A. Christ is an unfailing friend. He is "a friend that sticketh closer than a brother" (Prov. 18:24).

B. Christ is dependable and trustworthy. We should follow his example, be true to God, true to others, and true to ourselves.

IV. Christ Is Undaunted

"Nay, in all these things we are more than conquerors through him that loved us" (Rom. 8:37).
A. Christ kept the faith, completing his purpose. He was undaunted by persecution, ridicule, and even death.
B. We are conquerors through Christ. We must keep on keeping on when trials, troubles, and testings strike. Like Christ we must never give up (*see* Phil. 4:13).

V. Christ Is Undefeated

"But thanks be to God, which giveth us the victory through our Lord Jesus Christ" (1 Cor. 15:57).
A. Christ arose from the dead, victorious over death, hell, and the grave (*see* 1 Cor. 15:55).
B. We can be victorious also. Jesus said, "Because I live, ye shall live also" (John 14:19). Emulating Christ brings victory in this life and eternal life in the world to come.

10

The Greatness of God's Love

"But God, who is rich in mercy, for his great love wherewith he loved us" (Eph. 2:4).

I. The "Who" of God's Love

"God is love" (1 John 4:8, 16).
A. God is the "who" of his love. He had no beginning and will have no ending. He is from everlasting to everlasting.
B. God's love is great because he is great. God created the heavens, the earth, and all that is contained therein.

II. The "What" of God's Love

"God so loved the world" (John 3:16).
A. The "what" of God's love refers to every person—the great and small, black and white, and rich and poor alike.
B. God's love includes the alcoholic, drug abuser, prostitute, terrorist. All who repent and forsake their sins may be saved.

III. The "Where" of God's Love

"Whither shall I go from thy spirit? or whither shall I flee from thy presence?" (Ps. 139:7).
A. The "where" of God's love refers to "everywhere." His love went to Calvary, where he atoned for the sins of the world.
B. God's love extends to the uttermost parts of the earth. It

reaches the haughty and proud and includes those in the depths of despair.

IV. The "When" of God's Love

"God commendeth his love toward us, in that, while we were yet sinners, Christ died for us" (Rom. 5:8).
A. The "when" of God's love means "at all times." God's love continues forever, for he is eternal.
B. Since God always was and always will be, his love is from everlasting to everlasting, for "God is love." "Yea, I have loved thee with an everlasting love" (Jer. 31:3).

V. The "Why" of God's Love

"Truly our fellowship is with the Father, and with his Son Jesus Christ" (1 John 1:3).
A. The "why" of God's love is beyond our comprehension. However, we do know that God desires to fellowship with his creation.
B. Because of his great love, God gave his only Son to die on the cross for our sins and to bring us back into fellowship with himself.

11

God's Way Is Best

"Commit thy way unto the LORD; trust also in him; and he shall bring it to pass" (Ps. 37:5).

I. The Relinquishment

"Commit thy way unto the LORD" (Ps. 37:5).

A. Some Christians insist on clinging to their own ways. They lack spiritual victory.

B. If we are to enjoy God's best, we must yield our way, will, work, and walk to him. "As ye have therefore received Christ Jesus the Lord, so walk ye in him" (Col. 2:6).

C. To walk in God's way and please him means we must totally commit our time, talent, and treasure to him.

D. We should be ready to assist the needy and homeless, comfort the bereaved and lonely, sharing Christ with others whenever opportunity affords.

II. The Reliance

"Trust also in him" (Ps. 37:5).

A. Christians often fail to trust in the Lord as they should. They rely on their own strength and fail.

B. Some Christians depend too much on doctors, lawyers, or friends. We should be thankful for the help of others, but our ultimate trust must be in God.

C. We should trust in the Lord with our "whole spirit and soul and body" (1 Thess. 5:23). Bank accounts may fail, money markets may fail, possessions may fail, but Jesus never fails.

D. God's way is best. The Scripture says, "And the LORD shall help them, and deliver them . . . because they trust in him" (Ps. 37:40).

III. The Reward

"And he shall bring it to pass" (Ps. 37:5).
A. God rewards those who are totally committed to him, who trust him implicitly. "He will make your righteousness shine like the dawn, the justice of your cause like the noonday sun" (Ps. 37:6 NIV).
B. God rewards his children by enabling them to be a blessing to others. Their influence reaches out to attract others to Christ.
C. God's way is best. He not only rewards the faithful in this life, but he rewards them also in the next life eternally.
D. Jesus said, "I go to prepare a place for you. . . . I will come again, and receive you unto myself; that where I am, there ye may be also" (John 14:2, 3).

12

God's Word Is G-R-E-A-T

*"In the beginning was the Word, and the Word was with God,
and the Word was God" (John 1:1).*

I. G-racious Word

*"And the Word was made flesh, and dwelt among us" (John
1:14).*
A. Christ is the gracious Word who came down from
heaven to die on the cross for our sins, taking our place.
B. God's Word is great because "he was manifested to take
away our sins" (1 John 3:5). All who will repent, believe,
and forsake their sins may be saved.

II. R-eliable Word

*"Thy word is a lamp unto my feet, and a light unto my
path" (Ps. 119:105).*
A. People and possessions fail, but God's Word is trustworthy and dependable. It never fails.
B. The rich and poor, great and small, and young and old
may safely trust in God's Word (*see* Ps. 119:42).

III. E-nduring Word

*"Heaven and earth shall pass away, but my words shall not
pass away" (Matt. 24:35).*
A. There are few things in today's world that are enduring.
They wear out, rust, decay, or disappear.
B. God's Word is great because it is enduring. It doesn't
last for just a day, week, month, or year. God's Word is
eternal (*see* Ps. 119:160; Isa 40:8).

IV. A-uthentic Word

"All scripture is given by inspiration of God, and is profitable for doctrine, for reproof, for correction, for instruction in righteousness" (2 Tim. 3:16).

A. *Authentic* means: "That which can be believed or accepted . . . genuine; real . . . authoritative"—Webster.

B. God's Word is great. He gave his Word to faithful men who recorded and preserved it. His Word has stood the test of skepticism, misuse, and abuse. It has never failed (*see* Ps. 119:89, 90).

V. T-imely Word

" . . . that we through patience and comfort of the scriptures might have hope" (Rom. 15:4).

A. God's Word is effective for all people, in all places, and at all times. It is no less potent today than when it was first recorded.

B. God's Word is great because it is "quick and powerful" in the now (Heb. 4:12). The promises bring pardon, purity, peace, and purpose to those who trust and obey (*see* Ps. 119:11).

13

Grow Up in Christ

"But speaking the truth in love, may grow up into him in all things, which is the head, even Christ" (Eph. 4:15).

I. Grow Up Concerning Possessions

"A man's life consisteth not in the abundance of the things he possesseth" (Luke 12:15).
A. Many Christians place too much value on money and possessions.
B. It isn't wrong to have money, but we must heed the scriptural warning: "The love of money is the root of all evil" (1 Tim. 6:10).
C. We grow up concerning possessions when we give God first place (*see* Matt. 6:33).

II. Grow Up Concerning Pleasure

" . . . lovers of pleasures more than lovers of God" (2 Tim. 3:4).
A. We live in a pleasure-seeking, pleasure-loving society. Billions of dollars are spent on pleasure yearly. People are searching for fun more than for God.
B. The greatest pleasure possible is knowing Christ. He offers real and lasting enjoyment and satisfies the longing soul (*see* Ps. 107:9).
C. Grow up concerning pleasure. Be faithful in prayer and the ministry of God's Word, and enjoy the fellowship of other Christians.

III. Grow Up Concerning Popularity

"How can ye believe, which receive honour one of another" (John 5:44).

A. It is natural to desire appreciation and the good will of others, but we should not seek exaltation and glory from them.
B. Popularity is usually short-lived. It can be here today and gone tomorrow.
C. Growing up concerning popularity means seeking to please and glorify God. His approval endures as long as we trust in him. (*see* Isa. 26:4).

IV. Grow Up Concerning Position

"Labour . . . for that meat which endureth unto everlasting life" (John 6:27).

A. Some Christians put too much importance on their position. They live, eat, and sleep for their jobs.
B. Work is necessary, but we must give God first place. Take time to do God's work, attend his house, and encourage others.
C. A glorious promotion awaits those who grow up in Christ. They will be promoted to a land that is fairer than day, eternal in the heavens (*see* Rev. 21:23).

14

How to Deal with Stress

"Take therefore no [anxious] thought for the morrow" (Matt. 6:34).

I. Concentrate on Things That Are Calming

"Whatsoever things are lovely . . . of good report . . . think on these things" (Phil. 4:8).

A. Today's society is caught up in noise and confusion. Its music is loud and thunderous; its entertainment is explosive, sometimes destructive.

B. Deal with stress by concentrating on calming influences. Fellowship with nature. The hills, valleys, and streams bring relaxation.

C. Listen to the soothing hymns of the church. Pray and fellowship with God while meditating on his promises.

II. Cooperate with Inevitable Conditions

"And we know that in all things God works for the good of those who love him" (Rom. 8:28 NIV).

A. Many Christians suffer stress because they struggle with and fight against inevitable conditions.

B. Jesus conquered stress because he did not fret about difficult situations. He simply turned impossibilities into opportunities. We should do likewise.

C. Sometimes we must accept situations that we are powerless to change, doing our best and trusting God for the rest.

III. Comfort Others Who Have Complaints

"Who comforteth us . . . that we may be able to comfort them which are in any trouble" (2 Cor. 1:4).
A. Many Christians fail to comfort others as they should. They are too concerned about selfish interests.
B. Jesus cared about the difficulties of others. He healed the sick, gave sight to the blind, and forgave the sinful.
C. We should get involved in helping the less fortunate also. Comforting others who have problems will also help to solve our own complaints.

IV. Constantly Trust God with All Concerns

"Trust in him at all times" (Ps. 62:8).
A. If we are to conquer stress, we should be aware of God's presence at all times. We do not always feel his presence, but through faith we know he is near.
B. We are able to trust God because we are not alone. He promised, "I will never leave thee, nor forsake thee" (Heb. 13:5). Practice the presence of God.
C. We must also yield ourselves to God's will, letting him do his work through us, carrying the responsibility (*see* Rom. 6:13).

15

How to Be More Than Conquerors

"Nay, in all these things we are more than conquerors through him that loved us" (Rom. 8:37).

I. Conquer with More Prayer

"But in every thing by prayer . . . let your requests be made known unto God" (Phil. 4:6).

A. Many Christians lack victory because they neglect to pray. Some pray about the big things that happen but forget that it is "the little foxes, that spoil the vines" (Song of Sol. 2:15).

B. If we are to be more than conquerors, we must pray about everything, both the small and great, continuing always in prayer. The Scripture admonishes, "Pray without ceasing" (1 Thess. 5:17).

II. Conquer with More Promises

"For all the promises of God in him are yea, and in him Amen, unto the glory of God by us" (2 Cor. 1:20).

A. Some Christians falter when it comes to reading, remembering, and relying on God's promises. They unsuccessfully depend on their own strength.

B. If we are to be more than conquerors, we must trust God and depend on his promises. The Scripture says, "There hath not failed one word of all his good promise" (1 Kings 8:56).

III. Conquer with More Peace

"And the peace of God . . . shall keep your hearts and minds" (Phil. 4:7).

A. Some Christians fail to be victorious because they lack God's peace. They live with fear and doubts rather than with faith and confidence.
B. If we are to be more than conquerors, we must partake of God's peace. Jesus said, "My peace I give unto you. . . . Let not your heart be troubled" (John 14:27). We must simply accept the peace he offers.

IV. Conquer with More Praise

"But I will hope continually, and will yet praise thee more and more" (Ps. 71:14).

A. Many Christians are remiss when it comes to praising the Lord. They wear long faces, possess negative attitudes, and lack victory.
B. If we are to be more than conquerors, we must praise the Lord more. The psalmist said, "While I live I will praise the LORD: I will sing praises unto my God while I have any being" (Ps. 146:2). He also said, "I will bless the LORD at all times: his praise shall continually be in my mouth" (Ps. 34:1).

16

How the Lord Helps His People

*"God is our refuge and strength, a very present help in trou-
ble" (Ps. 46:1).*

I. He Speaks Through Prevailing Prayer

*"He shall call upon me, and I will answer him" (Ps.
91:15).*
A. Webster defines *prevail*: "To produce or achieve the
   desired effect; to be effective; succeed."
B. We are effective when we fellowship with God. He
   speaks to us and answers our prayers.
C. Christians should continue in a spirit of prayer at all
   times. Jesus said, "Men ought always to pray and not to
   faint" (Luke 18:1).

II. He Assures Through Precious Promises

*"Whereby are given unto us exceeding great and precious
promises: that by these ye might be partakers of the divine
nature" (2 Peter 1:4).*
A. Many Christians neglect the promises of God. Through
   busyness with other concerns, they forfeit the benefits of
   God's Word.
B. God's precious promises assure Christians of his protec-
   tion and provision.
C. God helps his people through the assurance of his
   promises. We must read them, review them, reflect, and
   rely on them.

III. He Calms Through Personal Peace

"Peace I leave with you, my peace I give unto you" (John 14:27).

A. Today's world is overrun with illicit sex, drug abuse, and terrorism. Millions are searching unsuccessfully for peace.

B. Real and lasting peace is found only in Jesus Christ. He offers peace to those who obey and trust him.

C. Jesus said, "My peace I give unto you" (John 14:27). Accept his personalized peace today.

IV. He Assists Through Providential Power

"And we know that in all things God works for the good of those who love him" (Rom. 8:28 NIV).

A. Christians are subject to trials, troubles, and testing like everyone else. They are not exempt simply because they know Christ.

B. God helps his people through providential means. He works everything (good and bad) together for their benefit and his glory (*see* Rom. 8:28).

C. God often rescues his own. At times he sends his angels to assist. "For he shall give his angels charge over thee, to keep thee in all thy ways" (Ps. 91:11).

17

Live for Christ Today

"He died for all, that they which live should not henceforth live unto themselves, but unto him which died for them, and rose again" (2 Cor. 5:15).

I. Look to Christ Today

"Looking unto Jesus the author and finisher of our faith . . ." (Heb. 12:2).

A. Many Christians look to doctors, lawyers, ministers, or friends more than they look to Christ; they find disappointment.

B. While help from others should be appreciated, real and lasting help can come only from the Lord. "Therefore I will look unto the Lord" (Micah 7:7).

II. Learn from Christ Today

"Let the word of Christ dwell in you richly in all wisdom" (Col. 3:16).

A. Some Christians neglect the Word of Christ. They are too involved with personal pursuits.

B. If we are to live for Christ today, we must read and meditate on his Word, which teaches us how to live victoriously over sin, self, and Satan (*see* Rom. 15:4).

III. Lean on Christ Today

"Trust in the LORD with all thine heart; and lean not unto thine own understanding" (Prov. 3:5).

A. Christians fail when they lean on their own power, position, or possessions.

B. We must trust in Christ today. He enables us to accomplish our tasks and bear our responsibilities. "And the LORD shall help them" (Ps. 37:40).

IV. Lift with Christ Today

"We then, as workers together with him . . ." (2 Cor. 6:1).
A. When it comes to doing God's work, many Christians falter because of a lack of cooperation from others.
B. We are not alone. Christ is with us, beside us, and within us. He will enable us to assist the less fortunate, comfort the sick and lonely, and witness to the unsaved about Christ (*see* Phil. 4:13).

V. Love as Christ Today

"And walk in love, as Christ also hath loved us, and hath given himself for us" (Eph. 5:2).
A. Christ loved us so much he died on the cross, taking our place. We must love God and others also (*see* 1 John 4:11).
B. To live for Christ today we should look to him, learn from him, lean on him, lift with him, and love as he loves.

18

"Looking unto Jesus"

"Looking unto Jesus the author and finisher of our faith . . . "
(Heb. 12:2).

I. Look to Jesus *in* Everything

"For in him we live, and move, and have our being" (Acts 17:28).
A. Many Christians are ready to look to Jesus when trouble strikes, but when everything is going well, they lean on their own finite strength and fail.
B. We must look to Jesus in everything—in good times as well as bad, in joy as well as sorrow, and in triumph as well as trial.
C. The Scripture admonishes us to look to Jesus "that we may obtain mercy, and find grace to help in time of need" (Heb. 4:16).

II. Look to Jesus *for* Everything

"And whatsoever ye shall ask in my name, that will I do" (John 14:13).
A. Some Christians do not depend on the Lord to supply all their needs. They rely on self-effort and other people. They come to disappointment.
B. We should look to Jesus for life, love, food, clothing, and shelter—everything.
C. We are promised ample supply for all our needs, "according to his riches in glory by Christ Jesus" (Phil. 4:19).

III. Look to Jesus *with* Everything

"And I pray God your whole spirit and soul and body be preserved blameless" (1 Thess. 5:23).

A. Some Christians fail to totally look to Jesus. They reserve a portion of their life for self.
B. If we're to be victorious, we must look to Jesus with everything—time, talent, and treasure. We must be totally dedicated to him.
C. Paul urged us to "present your bodies a living sacrifice, holy, acceptable unto God" (Rom. 12:1).

IV. Look to Jesus *Through* Everything

"After that ye have suffered a while . . . stablish, strengthen, settle you" (1 Peter 5:10).

A. Christians may look to Jesus during happy times, but complain and even blame God when suffering strikes.
B. God often allows suffering to strengthen our faith and fulfill his purpose. We must continue to look to Jesus and seek his purpose with patience and trust.
C. When traveling through valley experiences, Peter advised, "But rejoice, inasmuch as ye are partakers of Christ's sufferings" (1 Peter 4:13).

19

The Measure of God's Mercy

"Hear me, O LORD; for thy lovingkindness is good: turn unto me according to the multitude of thy tender mercies" (Ps. 69:16).

I. God's Mercy Reaches Upward

"For as the heaven is high above the earth, so great is his mercy toward them that fear him" (Ps. 103:11).
A. God's mercy reaches upward, beyond man's exploration of outer space. The rich and proud are included.
B. Presidents, kings, and generals—all those who humble themselves and accept Christ as Savior and Lord—may be saved.
C. The Scripture admonishes, "O give thanks unto the God of heaven: for his mercy endureth for ever" (Ps. 136:26).

II. God's Mercy Reaches Downward

"Who remembered us in our low estate: for his mercy endureth for ever" (Ps. 136:23).
A. God's mercy is great and good. It reaches downward to the discouraged, distressed, and depressed.
B. God's mercy accepts all who forsake their sins with simple, trusting faith.
C. God's mercy reaches up to the proud and haughty and down to the lowest, setting them on the same level, when they become one in Christ.

III. God's Mercy Reaches Inward

"Let, I pray thee, thy merciful kindness be for my comfort. . . . Let thy tender mercies come unto me" (Ps. 119:76, 77).

A. God's tender mercy reaches inward to the heart, mind, and soul, bringing comfort and contentment.
B. God's mercy feels with compassion and love. It cheers the bereaved and lonely and heals the brokenhearted.
C. God's tender mercies reach inward, exchanging our sorrow for his joy. His stability replaces our frustration and changes our disappointments to his appointments (*see* Ps. 136:23, 24).

IV. God's Mercy Reaches Outward

"The earth, O LORD, is full of thy mercy: teach me thy statutes" (Ps. 119:64).
A. God's mercy extends outward to the whole world. It reaches the great and small, black and white, rich and poor, old and young alike.
B. All who repent of their sins and believe in Christ may be saved at all times, in all places (*see* Eph. 2:4).
C. "O give thanks unto the God of gods . . . for his mercy endureth for ever" (Ps. 136:2, 3).

20

P-O-W-E-R of God's Word

"The word of God is quick, and powerful, and sharper than any twoedged sword" (Heb. 4:12).

I. P-enetrating Power

"The word of God . . . piercing even to the dividing asunder of soul and spirit . . . " (Heb. 4:12).

A. God's Word penetrates the heart of sinners. It brings forgiveness to those who repent and believe.

B. God's Word penetrates the hearts of his people who are loaded down with burdens. It provides comfort to his trusting children (*see* Ps. 119:165).

II. O-vercoming Power

"And Jesus answered . . . Get thee behind me, Satan: for it is written . . . " (Luke 4:8).

A. When Jesus was tempted forty days in the wilderness, he overcame through the power of God's Word.

B. We must depend on God's Word to overcome the onslaught of the enemy also. Like Paul, we can be "more than conquerors through him that loved us" (Rom. 8:37).

III. W-onderworking Power

"Nevertheless at thy word I will let down the net" (Luke 5:5).

A. Peter obeyed Christ's Word and the miracle happened. The overflow broke the fishing net. Two ships were filled with fish.

B. The power of God's Word is the same today. Jesus said, "If ye abide in me, and my words abide in you, ye shall ask what ye will, and it shall be done" (John 15:7).

IV. E-verlasting Power

"Heaven and earth shall pass away, but my words shall not pass away" (Matt. 24:35).
A. In today's society few things are lasting. Temporal possessions deteriorate.
B. The power of God's Word endures. Guns, tanks, not even nuclear power, can destroy it. "For ever, O Lord, thy word is settled in heaven" (Ps. 119:89).

V. R-evealing Power

"The word of God . . . is a discerner of the thoughts and intents of the heart" (Heb. 4:12).
A. God's Word reveals his will for humankind. It reveals his love and offers the promise of salvation to those who repent and believe on Jesus Christ.
B. It reveals the Holy Spirit who cleanses, empowers, and directs totally committed Christians. "He will guide you into all truth" (John 16:13).

47

21

R-I-C-H Through Christ

"That in the ages to come he might shew the exceeding riches of his grace in his kindness toward us through Christ Jesus" (Eph. 2:7).

I. Rich in R-edemption

"In whom we have redemption through his blood . . . according to the riches of his grace" (Eph. 1:7).
A. Humankind disobeyed God, fell from grace, and became spiritually bankrupt.
B. Because of God's great love, Jesus gave himself to die on the cross, thus paying the penalty for our sins (*see* John 3:16).
C. We can become rich in redemption when we repent and receive Christ by faith.

II. Rich in I-nstruction

"Let the word of Christ dwell in you richly in all wisdom" (Col. 3:16).
A. Many Christians lack spiritual victory because they neglect God's Word.
B. Christ leads, guides, and directs through his Word, making us rich in instruction.
C. The psalmist said, "I will meditate in thy precepts. . . . I will delight myself in thy statutes: I will not forget thy word" (Ps. 119:15, 16).

III. Rich in C-ontentment

"But godliness with contentment is great gain" (1 Tim. 6:6).

A. Today's world is filled with discontented people who are dissatisfied with their jobs, houses, cars, money, and marriages.
B. Many Christians lack contentment. They fail to trust God and give him first place. "But seek ye first the kingdom of God" (Matt. 6:33).
C. Real and lasting contentment is found only in Christ. The psalmist said, "For he satisfieth the longing soul" (Ps. 107:9).

IV. Rich in H-eirship

"And if children, then heirs; heirs with God, and joint-heirs with Christ . . ." (Rom. 8:17).
A. We can be free from condemnation if we "walk not after the flesh, but after the Spirit" (Rom. 8:1).
B. Totally committed Christians are cleansed and filled with God's love, joy, and peace. They are rich in heirship through Christ.
C. Spirit-filled Christians work, witness, and walk in God's way. "For as many as are led by the Spirit of God, they are the sons of God" (Rom. 8:14).

22

Say *No* to Discouragement

"Why art thou cast down, O my soul? and why art thou disquieted in me? hope thou in God" (Ps. 42:5).

I. Return to the Lord

"Return unto me, and I will return unto you, saith the LORD of hosts" Mal. 3:7).

A. When discouraged, many Christians drift away from the Lord, neglecting prayer, God's Word, and church attendance.

B. God's Word admonishes, "Draw nigh to God, and he will draw nigh to you" (James 4:8).

C. Say *no* to discouragement. Return unto the Lord. Revive your prayer life and Bible meditation. Restore your church attendance and support.

II. Radiate for the Lord

"Let your light so shine before men, that they may see your good works" (Matt. 5:16).

A. Radiate means "to give forth or spread happiness, love" —Webster.

B. When discouragement strikes, some Christians spread gloom and doom. They see only the bad in others, the church, and in circumstances.

C. Say *no* to discouragement. Replace negatives with positives. Look for the good, not the bad.

III. Rely on the Lord

"Commit thy way unto the LORD; trust also in him; and he shall bring it to pass" (Ps. 37:5).

A. Some Christians rely on temporal possessions more than on God. Others rely too much on people. They come to disappointment.
B. "It is good for me to draw near to God: I have put my trust in the Lord GOD, that I may declare all thy works," said the psalmist (Ps. 73:28).
C. Say *no* to discouragement. Rely on the Lord. Depend on him. He never disappoints or fails.

IV. Rejoice in the Lord

"Rejoice in the LORD alway: and again I say, Rejoice" (Phil. 4:4).

A. Many Christians fall into discouragement because they fail to offer enough praise to God. They are too involved with selfish pursuits.
B. It is difficult, if not impossible, to rejoice in the Lord and be discouraged at the same time.
C. The psalmist said, "I will bless the LORD at all times" (Ps. 34:1). Say *no* to discouragement. Rejoice in the Lord today.

23

Strength for Each Day

"And as thy days, so shall thy strength be" (Deut. 33:25).

I. Strength Through Prayer to God

"And all things, whatsoever ye shall ask in prayer, believing, ye shall receive" (Matt. 21:22).
A. Many Christians lack strength because they are remiss where their prayer life is concerned.
B. Prayer is the Christian's lifeline. Through prayer we communicate and fellowship with God.
C. The Scripture admonishes, "But in everything by prayer . . . let your requests be made known unto God" (Phil. 4:6).

II. Strength Through the Promises of God

"I will strengthen thee; yea, I will help thee" (Isa. 41:10).
A. Some Christians lack strength because they neglect the promises of God.
B. We should seek out the promises in God's Word that fit our needs, remember them, recall them often, and claim them as our own.
C. We have been given "exceeding great and precious promises: that by these ye might be partakers of the divine nature" (2 Peter 1:4).

III. Strength Through Performance for God

"I can do all things through Christ which strengtheneth me" (Phil. 4:13).

A. Christians gain strength by doing God's work. He enables them to accomplish tasks that bless others and glorify him.
B. Many people fail to do God's work because they are too involved with their own interests.
C. Take time for God. He promised "power to the faint; and to them that have no might he increaseth strength" (Isa. 40:29).

IV. Strength Through Praise to God

"But I will hope continually, and will yet praise thee more and more. . . . I will go in the strength of the Lord God" (*Ps. 71:14, 16*).

A. After saying he would praise the Lord more and more, the psalmist said, "I will go in the strength of the Lord."
B. We gain strength by praising the Lord. Praise encourages a positive attitude, and lifts our sagging spirits.
C. God is worthy of all our praise. We can never praise him enough. The psalmist said, "His praise shall continually be in my mouth" (Ps. 34:1).

24

The Greatest Text

*"God so loved the world, that he gave his only begotten Son,
that whosoever believeth in him should not perish, but have
everlasting life" (John 3:16).*

I. The Greatest Love

"God so loved the world . . ." (John 3:16).
A. Children may have great love for their parents and pets.
   Parents may have greater love for their spouses and children, but God's love is greatest.
B. God's love is the greatest because of its purpose. It
   delivers from sin, heals hurts and disappointments, and
   mends broken hearts and homes.
C. It reaches upward to the proud, downward to the
   depressed, inward to the affections, and outward to all
   humankind (*see* John 3:1).

II. The Greatest Gift

". . . that he gave his only begotten Son" (John 3:16).
A. Many great gifts are given—houses, cars, money. Even
   greater gifts are education, respect, appreciation, and
   love.
B. God gave the greatest gift: "his only begotten Son."
   Kings, presidents, not even angels, could atone for our
   sins. Only Christ's blood was efficacious.
C. Jesus Christ is the greatest gift because he forgives sins,
   cleanses hearts, gives peace and eternal life to all who
   repent and believe (*see* 2 Cor. 9:15).

III. The Greatest Faith

*". . . that whosoever believeth in him should not perish"
(John 3:16).*

A. Many Christians believe God for divine healing and mountain-moving miracles. Faith is pleasing to God (*see* Heb. 11:6).

B. The greatest faith involves believing in Jesus Christ as Savior and Lord. Through faith we receive God's greatest gift.

C. Through faith we live and overcome. "And this is the victory . . . even our faith" (1 John 5:4).

IV. The Greatest Life

". . . but have everlasting life" (John 3:16).

A. History records many who have sacrificed their lives to benefit mankind: Livingstone, Taylor, Barton.

B. The greatest life is "everlasting life." It is available to all who accept God's greatest love and gift.

C. Everlasting life can begin now and continue forever. Nothing can separate us from the love of God (*see* Rom. 8:35-39).

25

Waiting Brings Help from God

"Our soul waiteth for the LORD: he is our help and our shield" (Ps. 33:20).

I. Waiting Brings Strength from God

"But they that wait upon the LORD shall renew their strength" (Isa. 40:31).

A. Some Christians lack the strength they need to be a blessing to others. They unsuccessfully depend on self-effort.

B. God wants to use our time, talents, and treasures. We must wait on him, trusting him for needed strength.

C. The psalmist advised: "Wait on the LORD: be of good courage, and he shall strengthen thine heart: wait, I say, on the LORD" (Ps. 27:14).

II. Waiting Brings Serenity from God

"Rest in the LORD, and wait patiently for him: fret not thyself" (Ps. 37:7).

A. There is little peace and quiet in today's world. Noise, strife, and distraction are the order.

B. Many Christians fail to rest in the Lord and wait for him. They lead complicated lives.

C. We must take time to get quiet before the Lord. God's Word admonishes: "Be still, and know that I am God" (Ps. 46:10).

III. Waiting Brings Stability from God

"I waited patiently for the LORD; and he . . . set my feet upon a rock, and established my goings" (Ps. 40:1, 2).

A. Many people lack stability in their Christian walk. They are up one day and down the next. Their influence is hurt and their outreach for God is limited.
B. We must wait patiently on the Lord in prayer and the study of his Word, trusting him to stabilize our lives.
C. God wants his children to become established in the faith. He promised, "After that ye have suffered a while . . . stablish, strengthen, settle you" (1 Peter 5:10).

IV. Waiting Brings Submission to God

"And he . . . kneeled down, and prayed . . . nevertheless not my will, but thine, be done" (Luke 22:41, 42).
A. In perhaps his most excruciating hour Jesus waited in prayer. He yielded his will to his heavenly Father's will.
B. We must wait on the Lord, submitting our will to God as Jesus did. God's will is always best.
C. We should surrender all to God, totally committing our lives to him—physically, mentally, and spiritually.

26

"We Ought to O-B-E-Y God"

"We ought to obey God rather than men" (Acts 5:29).

I. O-ffer Praise to God

"Offer unto God thanksgiving; and pay thy vows to the most High" (Ps. 50:14).

A. Some Christians are ready to give honor and glory to other people, but fail to give it to God.
B. We obey God when we thank him. God is worthy of all our praise. We can never praise him sufficiently.
C. The psalmist said, "I will bless the LORD at all times: his praise shall continually be in my mouth" (Ps. 34:1).

II. B-elieve the Promises of God

"Who through faith subdued kingdoms, wrought righteousness, obtained promises" (Heb. 11:33).

A. Many Christians fail to exercise faith in the promises. If they read them, they fail to remember and recall them.
B. Peter and the other apostles believed and practiced the words that Christ gave them. "They ceased not to teach and preach Jesus Christ" (Acts 5:42).
C. In order to obey God, we must believe his promises. They "were written for our learning, that we through patience and comfort of the scriptures might have hope" (Rom. 15:4).

III. E-njoy the Peace of God

"And the peace of God . . . shall keep your hearts and minds" (Phil. 4:7).

A. Our world is filled with hatred, strife, and evil of many kinds. Millions of people unsuccessfully seek for peace.
B. Many Christians lack peace, also. They worry and fret instead of accepting God's peace.
C. We must look to God for real and lasting peace. We please the Lord when we accept his peace. Jesus said, "Peace I leave with you, my peace I give unto you" (John 14:27).

IV. Y-ield to the Purpose of God

"Yield yourself unto God" (Rom. 6:13).
A. Many people do not yield to God's purpose. They are too consumed with selfish and personal goals.
B. If we obey God, we must surrender, exchanging our desires for his purpose, our will for his will, and our way for his way. They are best.
C. We promote God's purpose when we assist the needy, comfort the lonely, and witness to the unsaved about God's saving and sustaining power (*see* Heb. 5:9).

27

What It Means to Be a Christian

"And the disciples were called Christians first in Antioch"
(Acts 11:26).

I. We Must Receive Christ

"Therefore if any man be in Christ, he is a new creature"
(2 Cor. 5:17).
A. To become a Christian means receiving Christ. It includes repenting, believing, and forsaking our sins. Jesus said, "Except ye repent, ye shall all likewise perish" (Luke 13:3, 5).
B. Receiving Christ means being in him. "Old things are passed away" (2 Cor. 5:17). Old friends, habits, and sinful pursuits drop off.
C. In Christ "all things are become new" (v. 17). We receive a new life, faith, hope, love, joy, and peace.

II. We Must Resemble Christ

". . . leaving us an example, that we should follow his steps" (1 Peter 2:21).
A. As Christians we should emulate Christ in our thinking, seeing, hearing, speaking, doing, and going.
B. We should look for the positive and good; be kind, compassionate, and understanding (*see* Col. 3:12, 13).
C. As Christians, we should work with diligence and purpose, setting our affections on things above (*see* Col. 3:1, 2).

III. We Must Represent Christ

"And ye shall be witnesses unto me" (Acts 1:8).

A. As Christians, we are to represent Christ at home, school, work, and play—everywhere. We should seek to exemplify him in deed and conversation.

B. Missionaries are to represent Christ on foreign fields. They speak and witness for him. We should do the same here at home.

C. We can represent Christ by giving words of encouragement, good deeds, and witnessing to the unsaved about him (*see* Isa. 43:10).

IV. We Shall Reign with Christ

"And so shall we ever be with the Lord" (1 Thess. 4:17).

A. Those who receive Christ, resemble Christ, represent Christ, shall also reign with Christ.

B. The Scripture says, "When Christ, who is our life, shall appear, then shall ye also appear with him in glory" (Col. 3:4).

C. Being a Christian means that we are in Christ, like Christ, for Christ, and with Christ for now and throughout eternity.

28

Win the Christian R-A-C-E

"Let us run with patience the race that is set before us, looking unto Jesus" (Heb. 12:1, 2).

I. R-each Forward with Persistence

". . . reaching forth unto those things which are before" (Phil. 3:13).
A. Some Christians live in the past. They spend much time dwelling on things that have already happened.
B. As Christians we must emulate Paul and forget "the things which are behind" (v. 13).
C. We can win the Christian race by persistently "reaching forth unto those things which are before" (v. 13) and "looking unto Jesus" (Heb. 12:2).

II. A-pply Yourself with Purpose

"I press toward the mark for the prize of the high calling of God" (Phil. 3:14).
A. Too many Christians lack purpose. They simply drift along aimlessly without thought of advancing the kingdom of God.
B. If we win the Christian race we must look to the future, making plans that will glorify the Lord.
C. We should take inventory of our spiritual life. Then, setting goals for overcoming our weaknesses, we should live with purpose.

III. C-onquer Evil with God's Power

"Nay, in all these things we are more than conquerors through him that loved us" (Rom. 8:37).

A. Today's world is filled with sin and evil. Satan is constantly trying to defeat God's people.
B. When their faith is tested, some Christians give up in despair. They fail to make use of God's conquering power.
C. We can win the Christian race with divine strength. Through prayer, the promises, and participation in God's work we can be "more than conquerors."

IV. E-ndure Hardness with Patience

"Endure hardness, as a good soldier of Jesus Christ" (2 Tim. 2:3).
A. Some Christians try to go to heaven on flowery beds of ease. Their lack of patience and endurance brings them to disappointment.
B. A good soldier must endure hardship. He must press forward even when the going is tough. We must "endure hardness, as a good soldier of Jesus Christ" also.
C. If we win the Christian race, we must be patient when testings and trials come. We trust God and keep on keeping on (*see* Matt. 24:13).